First World War
and Army of Occupation
War Diary
France, Belgium and Germany

2 DIVISION
99 Infantry Brigade
Trench Mortar Battery
1 November 1915 - 31 December 1915

WO95/1373/2

The Naval & Military Press Ltd
www.nmarchive.com
Published in association with The National Archives

Published by

The Naval & Military Press Ltd

Unit 10 Ridgewood Industrial Park,
Uckfield, East Sussex,
TN22 5QE England
Tel: +44 (0) 1825 749494

www.naval-military-press.com
www.nmarchive.com

This diary has been reprinted in facsimile from the original. Any imperfections are inevitably reproduced and the quality may fall short of modern type and cartographic standards.

© Crown Copyright
Images reproduced by permission of The National Archives, London, England, 2015.

Contents

Document type	Place/Title	Date From	Date To
Heading	WO95/1373 2 Div 99 Infantry Bde Trench Movers Battery.		
Heading	2 Div. 99 Bde 99 Trench Mortar Bty 1915 Oct To 1915 Dec.1042		
Heading	99th Trench Mortar Batty Vol I Oct 15		
Miscellaneous	War Diary 99th Trench Mortar Battery 81st Brigade 27th Division.		
Heading	99 Trench Motar Batty Nov Vol II		
War Diary	Ailly Sur Somme	01/11/1915	05/11/1915
War Diary	Pont Noyelles	05/11/1915	09/11/1915
War Diary	Meaulte	09/11/1915	09/11/1915
War Diary	Sector D1	14/11/1915	30/11/1915
Heading	99th Trench Motar Batty Dec Vol. III		
War Diary		01/12/1915	31/12/1915

WO95/1373
2 Div
99 Infantry Bde
Trench mortar Battery

~~3 Army Troops~~
2 DIV. 99 BDE.

99

TRENCH MORTAR BTY

1915 Oct to 1915 Dec

(1042)

27 · · 121/7341

81 at Bela.

3rd Army

99th Trench Mortar Batty.

Vol I

Oct 15

Oct

War Diary.
99th Trench Mortar Battery.
81st Brigade
27th Division.

Oct. 12th. Arrived at CHUIGNES.
" 14th. Received 29 rounds.
" 15th. Got No 1 gun in position opposite house at extreme South of DONPIERRE. Started emplacement for No 2 Gun opposite left tree of row running North from DONPIERRE.
" 16th. Completed emplacement & dug in No 2 gun.
" 17th. Attempted to register No 1 gun but abandoned owing to mist after 1 round
" 18th. Enemy's mortars opened fire at 3 P.M. I observed from listening post one mortar firing from house in centre of DONPIERRE Registered No 2 Gun on house.
1st Shot. Range 460 Fuse 12

Oct 18th. burst in the air.
2nd Shot. Same range fuse 14 burst in house and destroyed enemy's mortar and his ammunition. The house was practically destroyed.
Failing to observe position of the other enemy mortars we put 4 rounds in his 1st line of trenches. As he ceased firing then we did also.

" 19th. Received 30 rounds.
In reply to enemy's mortars fired 4 rounds into his 1st line 1 failed to explode. Destroyed 1 snipers post and a new sand-bag parapet. Landed last shot in trench which must have done some damage as he opened with a field battery. We ceased fire for fear he would locate our position.

" 20th Owing to mining operations we were forced to find new position. Started new emplacements. Were ordered to have guns

20th. ready to move by 4 P.M.
21st. inst.
21st. Guns & Ammunition out at
CHUIGNES. by 12 noon. Order postponed
till 2 end.
22nd Moved to WARFUSÉE
23rd Lieut. Miskie-Smith took over
command of Battery.
      G. D. Currie. 2/Lieut.
        1st East Surrey Reg t

23/31. Since taking command of
this Battery we have been
in rest at AILLY sur SOMME
      Martin K Smith Lt
        R F A (T)

27

99 French Motor Bain

No. 1 / Vol II

12/
7/21

G.H.G.

WAR DIARY
or
INTELLIGENCE SUMMARY
(Erase heading not required.)

Army Form C. 2118

Place	Date	Hour	Summary of Events and Information	Remarks and references to Appendices
AILLY sur SOMME	1/11/15 – 5/11/15		In rest with 27th Division.	
PONT. NOYELLES	5/11/15 – 9/11/15		Having been detached from 27th Division, this Battery, together with 96, 98 & 102 TMB's were embodied at X'th Corps Hd Qrs.	
MEAULTE	9/11/15		Battery arrived & was attached to 54th Infantry Brigade, 18th Division	
Sector D1.	14/11/15	11. am	Opened fire on enemy's 3rd line, who replied with "Sausage" mortars	
"	16/11/15	3.pm	In reply to enemy's fire, opened on 2nd line trenches, silencing them after 8 rounds.	
"	17/11/15	4.pm	In reply to enemy's fire opened on 1st & 2nd line trenches, one bomb falling into and blowing up a dug out.	
"	19/11/15	3.pm	Fired 8 rounds searching for enemy's "Sausage" mortar machine but failed to locate it, damaging their trenches.	
"	20/11/15		Day spent putting in posts to front which sank due to wet.	
"	24/10/15		Day quiet.	
"	25/11/15	11 am 3.50pm	Opened up. Searching for "Sausage" mortar. Eventually did caution – ater damage as enemy replied with Heavy & Light Artillery, "Sausages" "Oil drums" & rifle grenades. Nr 4 Bomb fired, did great damage. Evidently blowing up a German reserve store.	

WAR DIARY or INTELLIGENCE SUMMARY

Army Form C. 2118

(Erase heading not required.)

Instructions regarding War Diaries and Intelligence Summaries are contained in F.S. Regs., Part II. and the Staff Manual respectively. Title Pages will be prepared in manuscript.

Place	Date	Hour	Summary of Events and Information	Remarks and references to Appendices
Sector II 1.	23/11/15		Day passed quietly.	
"	24/11/15	3.30 p.m.	Enemy opened fire, evidently searching for the 2" mortars. Fired about 4 rounds, enemy increasing their firing; but after 1 more round they ceased fire. Later we fired 10 more rounds to which the enemy made but feeble reply.	
"	25/11/15	3.30 p.m.	Enemy mortars opened at 3.30 p.m. We fired 6 rounds silencing their mortars, but their field guns then opened on our position locating No. 2 Gun. Capt. Niven & 11th R. Fusiliers observers observing, reported that 11th round blew up a German dug out. Received a new position for No. 2 Gun & spent day dragging in & making dug outs etc. for ammunition.	
"	26/11/15			
"	27/11/15	5 p.m.	At request of Infantry, opened up in conjunction with 4" TMB to silence enemy, who were heavily bombarding our 2nd line. Enemy were using two "sausage" mortars, one of which I managed to locate from flashes. I immediately opened out on it, silencing it.	

Army Form C. 2118

WAR DIARY
or
INTELLIGENCE SUMMARY
(Erase heading not required.)

Instructions regarding War Diaries and Intelligence Summaries are contained in F. S. Regs., Part II. and the Staff Manual respectively. Title Pages will be prepared in manuscript.

Place	Date	Hour	Summary of Events and Information	Remarks and references to Appendices
Sector III.	28/4/15	3 p.m.	Bombarded enemy front line opposite "Enemy", smashing parapets. Fired 7 rounds. Fuzes very irregular, 4 rounds only finding their marks.	
"	29/4/15	12.15 pm	Enemy opened out with Shell mortars & Rifle Guns. Owing to trouble at Polk guns with adaptors & T. Tubes, delayed in replying. However at 12.35 got off 1 round, after which enemy ceased firing. During afternoon fired 4 rounds at triangle behind "Enemy" where enemy are supposed to have their Cook houses. One round threw up considerable quantity of wood. Another round landed in wood.	
"	30/4/15	12.15 pm	Enemy opened a heavy fire with field & large artillery. Our field guns replied but as bombardment continued I opened fire at 1.15pm. Silencing them after 10 rounds. It is significant that since our firing on them heavy ["Sausage"] mortar spotted on night of 27th that they have not again used this against this sector. I presume therefore that either a direct hit was made, or else the position learnt too hot for enemy. They have moved the mortar. No Sun

1875 Wt. W593/826 1,000,000 4/15 J.B.C. & A. A.D.S.S./Forms/C. 2118.

IV.

Army Form C. 2118

WAR DIARY
or
INTELLIGENCE SUMMARY
(Erase heading not required.)

Summary of Events and Information

Summary of Ammunition Expended.
November 1915

Rounds fired   83.
Days in Action   17
Average Rounds per day.   4.88.
No. of "Dud" Bombs.   7 or 8.43%.
Of these "Duds" Bombs.   5 were with the "Amatol" Bombs
                         2 "   "   "Ammonal" Bombs.

General Considerable difficulty has been experienced with
the new Adapters, which are of inferior Steel and bend. We are however
shortly to be supplied with the Enfield Rifle mechanism, with a
view to getting over this difficulty. In the mean time we are
being supplied with "T." Tubes friction, which were originally
used with three guns.

Martin V Smith
Lt.
R.F.A (T)

O.C. 99th Trench Mortar Battery
att. 18th Division

27 3rd army

99th General Staff Route

Dec / Vol III

WAR DIARY or INTELLIGENCE SUMMARY

Army Form C. 2118

(Erase heading not required.)

Instructions regarding War Diaries and Intelligence Summaries are contained in F. S. Regs., Part II. and the Staff Manual respectively. Title Pages will be prepared in manuscript.

Place	Date	Hour	Summary of Events and Information	Remarks and references to Appendices
	1/12/15		Rifle fire over during afternoon, rest of day quiet	
	2/12/15		Morning quite, took to drain (?) enemy's support. It was outranged by our guns.	
	3/12/15		Silenced (?) 2 ammunition dugouts fitted at work on their wire during evening. At request of infantry we fired 6 rounds & good 2 air bursts. 1 blind.	
	4/12/15		at work on dugouts.	
	5/12/15		Fired 6 rounds at support of infantry	
	6/12/15	3.30 P.M.	Fired 4 rounds at machine gun in front. Hit it with 3 rounds	
	7/12/15	2-30 P.M.	Fired 5 rounds. 1 air burst.	
		4-30 P.M.	Enemy opened fire & replied with 2 rounds	
	8/12/15	11 A.M.	Replied with 2 rounds to enemy's fire.	
	9/12/15		Quiet	
	10/12/15		Replied to enemy who fired 1 round from his last traverses. Traversing caused fire to cease & enemy did not reply & stopped all rifle fire.	for straightened line traversing
	11/12/15	11-40 A.M.	Fired 7 rounds (shrapnel) at support of infantry	
	12/12/15		Quiet	
	13/12/15		We fired 3 rounds (6 am's fire)	
	14/12/15		3 rounds fired during morning. Lt. K. Merritt O.C. Battery killed by sniper.	
	15/12/15	9 P.M.	We fired 2 rounds, night quiet.	
	16/12/15		2 air rounds fired, quiet.	
	17/12/15		6 rounds fired in reply to enemy trench mortars. The enemy shovelled our position	
	18/12/15		6 rounds fired in reply to enemy shrapnel of infantry 2/Lt J. Powell (Wilts Regt took over Bty.	
	19/12/15		Look out only gun is sent its to be overhauled. Position received a direct hit from	
	20/12/15		Enemy shell during evening knocking in emplacement rendering it unsafe.	
	21/12		Started work on our new emplacements carried on with them	
	30			
	31/12/15		Two guns in action in new positions, ready to fire when required by infantry	

J.R.P.